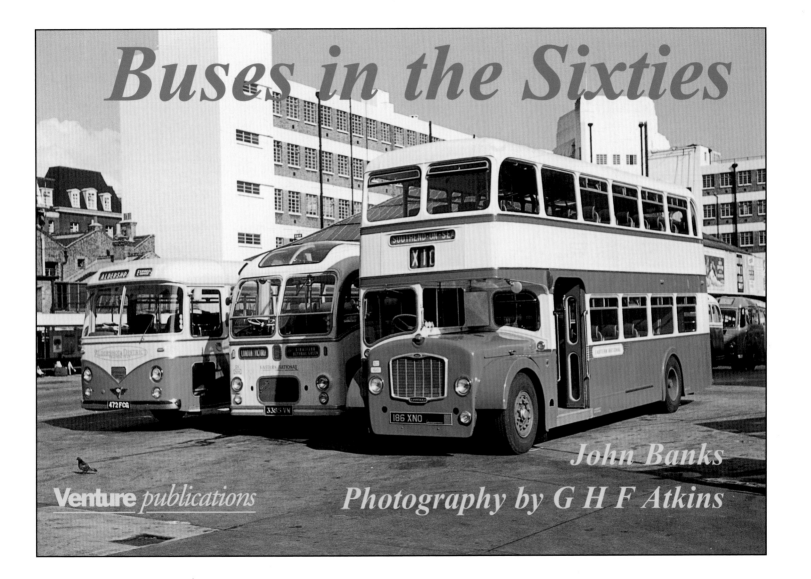

Buses in the Sixties

John Banks

Photography by G H F Atkins

Venture *publications*

Cover: In a busy April 1961 Nottingham scene, South Notts No. **73** (**CCK 651**) leads a Yorkshire Woollen District Beadle-Commer coach and a Trent double-decker out of the city. CCK 651, new to Ribble in 1949, had been with South Notts only since February 1961.

Rear Cover: There had been twin-steer six-wheeled single-deckers before the Bedford VAL, but the latter brought a new popularity to the type following its launch in the early nineteen-sixties. This one, bodied by Plaxton as a 52-seater, was **EDK 390D** in the Yelloway fleet. It was at Derby in March 1967. Behind, working on hire to Yelloway, was an example with an earlier style of Plaxton body.

Title page: BET (Aldershot & District, East Kent and Southdown) and BTC (Eastern National, including an impressive Bristol Lodekka for Southend-on-Sea) coaches lined up at Victoria Coach Station, epitomising medium distance express travel from London in the 1960s.

Below: The ubiquitous Bedford SB is represented by a 1960 example in the Skill's, of Nottingham, fleet, No. **23** (**23 HTO**). The Duple-bodied SB1 was parked ahead of a rarer bird in the shape of No. **51** (**551 BAU**), a Commer Avenger Mk IV with a TS3 two-stroke diesel engine and Plaxton coachwork. The Vauxhall Cresta car looks to be in Skill's livery, too. The picture was taken at Wollaton Street, Nottingham, in August 1964.

The company operators in our period were split between the British Electric Traction Group and the state-owned British Transport Commission fleets, also widely known simply as 'the Tilling fleets'. One of the most characterful of the BET operators was Southdown Motor Services, epitomised in this Pool Valley, Brighton view featuring Leyland PD2/12 Titans with Leyland - No. **729 (LUF 229)** - and Park Royal - No. **774 (OCD 774)** - bodies, taken on one of Geoffrey Atkins's all too rare visits south.

3

INTRODUCTION

What was it about the sixties? Variously described as 'sizzling', 'swinging' or 'sad' (to the followers of fashion, popular music or architecture) they had a rather different appeal for students of road passenger transport; for some, it was a rather bitter-sweet decade, especially for those born in the early 1940s, as was the writer, who thus had grown up during the heyday of the traditional, half-cab vehicle.

Small boys in the 1940s were teenagers in the 1950s: in neither era had the average lad a great deal of disposable income. Pennies spent on notebooks and pencils to record their observations of the local bus and coach scene (and, turned upside-down and starting from the back, steam locomotive numbers) were about the limit for many. But as the sixties took over from the fifties we were all ensconced in jobs of one sort or another. Onerous as this was to many a free and rebellious spirit, there was this to be said for being employed: it brought in wages. Parents had to have their cut, of course, for 'board and lodging', and girl-friends had to be taken to the cinema, but there was enough left from the wreck to finance eventually a cheap camera, a new film once a month or so and the odd photography expedition further afield than one's local bus station or coach park.

The new decade thus found young enthusiasts better placed to build up a photographic record of the road passenger transport scene at a time when much that was recognisable remained from the previous two decades. The late fifties, however, had seen the launch of the Leyland Atlantean, soon followed by the Daimler Fleetline, which between them altered the face of public transport in no small way. Bristol followed with the VR, but that didn't appear until the second half of the decade. The traditional bus - and strangely, not to say inconsistently, the underfloor-engined single-decker had by then been accepted as 'traditional' - carried on beyond the sixties, of course, but the decade in truth brought the end of it. Steam railway people were in the same boat: they began the decade with steam still a force in the land, and by the end of 1968 it had gone. So too on the road, it all came to an end on 31st December 1968 when that political monster the National Bus Company lurched into being and began to alter things: they were a long time a-dyin', though, NBC corporate liveries, for example, not appearing until well into the seventies.

At that time, as well as the 'war babies' with their Mirandas, Zenits and Praktikas - and more well-heeled souls armed with the products of Pentax, Canon and Olympus - a few senior figures in the transport photographer's hall of fame were still active, none more so than Nottingham's Geoffrey Atkins, who had been recording rail and road matters since 1927.

Geoffrey had developed a technique all his own. Born in 1912, he had in his formative years become fascinated by the art of the coachbuilder to such an extent that he wanted to make a career in coachbuilding. That would have meant a long apprenticeship and the chance did not come his way. In a subsequent remarkably stable career up to his retirement in 1977 he worked in Nottingham's City Treasurer's department, broken only by conscripted service in the RAF during the second world war.

Denied the opportunity to become a coachbuilder himself, Geoffrey did the next best thing by studying its development as a fascinated observer over the following three quarters of a century. And, better: he armed himself with a camera to make a photographic record of coachwork manufacturers' products. At first this was a modest Kodak vest pocket machine, which was soon replaced by the best upgrade he could afford. Geoffrey was one of that generation of enthusiastic amateur photographers who would never dream of taking their exposed films to the chemist for developing and printing. From the start he did all his own processing and quickly found that photography was a satisfying end in itself, as well as providing him with a visual record of his beloved coach and bus designs.

By the early 1930s his technique behind the lens had settled and he produced a quite stunning series of portraits of buses and coaches - not to mention steam locomotives - until the war and RAF service put a stop to transport photography for the duration. Not, however, before Geoffrey had tentatively experimented with early colour transparency film, from which emerged a mere handful of successful views.

The war over, he picked up where he had left off with his black and white work and the 1950s were as successful as had been the prewar decade in building up portraits of the coachbuilder's art. The 1960s - or at the very earliest, the late 1950s - were to tempt him once again to colour work; film was becoming more widely available, costs of using it were tumbling and this time the experiment led to consistently successful results throughout the sixties and seventies.

Working in black and white, Geoffrey had concentrated on individual vehicles in pictures composed to give him what he wanted as a representation of the coachbuilder's work; sometimes that meant a single view of a particular type of vehicle, at others more than one image was needed until the right one was 'in the can'. Only occasionally did Geoffrey record a wider view - general bus station views, for example, or street traffic scenes - in black and white; using colour transparency film, however, brought a change in his viewpoint and many superb general views - not a few of which appear in this book - were taken.

In an earlier book the writer described Geoffrey Atkins as the Eric Treacy of bus photographers; certainly in one major respect he and the Bishop were similar: neither was able to extend his photographic coverage to the south of England as much as he would have liked, apart from regular trips to London and very occasional holidays on the south coast.

Thus Geoffrey's colour work in the 1960s centres on Nottingham and the places he and his wife chose to take their holidays in that decade. These restraints nonetheless allowed the building up of a splendid archive, representative of most aspects of British bus and coach operation. Because colour work still took second place in quantity to monochrome, there are not enough images of any single company to fill a book; there are ample, however, to make a valued addition to the 'decade' series and a further volume of colour images devoted to the nineteen-seventies is planned.

It seems strange to representatives of the generation described at the head of these notes that the 'modern' 1960s, in which so much happened and our bus and coach world was stood on its head, are now forty years in the past. It was the last decade of the clear division of bus and coach operation into municipalities, BET companies, Tilling companies and independents.

Geoffrey Atkins first and foremost in that era followed the fortunes of the larger company operators; he had his favourites - among them Midland Red, Ribble, Crosville, United, West Yorkshire, Yorkshire Traction, Yorkshire Woollen, Lincolnshire, Midland General - some of which have been the subject of volumes in the *Prestige Series*, but was also at pains to record the activities of his two 'home' municipalities, Nottingham City Transport and West Bridgford Urban District Council (which towards the end of the decade were combined), and of London Transport, whose standard designs had fascinated him since the late nineteen-twenties and the old London General Omnibus Company.

Independents were by no means entirely neglected, particularly when their distinctive liveries seemed made for the still relatively new medium of colour transparency work: Barton and South Notts, both close at hand in Nottingham, spring to mind in this category.

They are all here, the companies' Leylands and Bristols, the municipalities' AECs, the independents' second-hand vehicles and their Bedford coaches; many of them have the engine at the front and had to be worked by a crew of two, features that will surely appeal to readers of the writer's generation.

The vehicle building factories and the coachbuilders were to undergo in the sixties as great an upheaval as did the industry they served. Mostly long-vanished now, Leyland and AEC, Guy and Bristol, Dennis and Crossley, Ford and Bedford, Commer and Sentinel, the home-made products of Midland Red and Barton were to be seen carrying bodywork from a bewildering variety of coachbuilders. To list the latter would be fruitless, but it is worth reminding ourselves that from their ranks such great names as Weymann, Park Royal, Roe, Burlingham, Willowbrook, Duple and Massey can no longer be seen as plates or transfers inside new public service vehicle bodywork.

The writer has, as so often before, had the willing and enthusiastic help of Ron Maybray and Philip Battersby in preparing caption material, and David and Mary Shaw have once again checked the proofs. John Senior has read the text and made several suggestions that have improved it considerably. Thank you all; and gratitude to The PSV Circle and The Omnibus Society, whose splendid publications are never far away when a book such as this one is in preparation.

Working on a book such as this necessarily exposes a writer to an attack of the 'rose-tinted spectacles' syndrome, an affliction to which the present scribe is particularly prone. In our hobby, as in many another, the 'Golden Age' is generally reckoned to be that in which one grew up and was first influenced by one's surroundings; naturally, therefore, it recedes farther into the past the older one becomes. In the 1960s the writer wondered what all the fuss was about when elder statesmen of the hobby spoke nostalgically of petrol-engined ADCs cruising silently along city streets in the 1920s and who, whilst not exactly disparaging the postwar Titans, Arabs and Regents, would have had us believe that such modern vehicles were a retrograde step. Looking out on today's sea of aquamarine and purple applied to buses 'that all look the same', my goodness! I know how they felt. Yes, the Regents and Titans were 'all the same', too, but they ran in what, subjectively, really were the good old days. There is nothing more certain than that today's young generation, in the year 2045, will hanker for the Optares and Tridents with which they are growing up.

Every photograph in this book and on its covers was taken by Geoffrey Atkins; Geoffrey's courteous and willing permission to use his best work is once more gratefully acknowledged by publisher and author. The support and encouragement given by Geoffrey to the writer, including responsibility for much of his collection, has brought a much closer involvement with and knowledge of Geoffrey's lifetime of photography, from which have arisen the twin satisfactions of bringing a comprehensive portfolio of Geoffrey's work to the enthusiast in affordable form and the greater one of witnessing Geoffrey's pleasure and enthusiasm as the library of our joint productions has grown.

Let, then, the camera of Geoffrey Atkins take us back, in a set of images that celebrates the end of the age of the half-cab as well as the first stirrings of what has become today's rear-engined, driver-only operated, deregulated scene; and let us be thankful that reliable, economical colour photography came in time for Geoffrey to provide such a splendid series of images.

Thank you, Geoffrey, from us all.

John Banks
Romiley, Cheshire, May 2002

In my ninetieth year - and almost exactly 75 years since I took my first bus photograph - I view with great satisfaction my collaboration with author John Banks, my friend for many years, in the various books which have appeared over the last two or three years using my photography. Bus photography has always been a most enjoyable hobby for me, but only a hobby, with all the constraints on time that that implies, and I am delighted that John, now responsible for the care and safety of my collection, has been able to do such a splendid job in making so much of my work available to the enthusiast in such a readily accessible and modestly priced format. I was very happy when I saw my colour work in this book, the first in the series: long may it continue.

G H F Atkins
Nottingham, July 2002

London's RT - a prewar design - had been thought rather sophisticated when it was the latest thing, but it was relatively simple in comparison with the Leyland Atlantean, of which London took an experimental batch of 50 (larger than many an operator's entire fleet) in 1965/6. They were found wanting and were outlasted by the RT. One of each at Victoria in March 1968.

In any volume based on the work of Geoffrey Atkins the bus and coach station at Huntingdon Street, Nottingham is bound to figure largely. It was not more than a mile or so from any of Geoffrey's addresses in the city over the years and it carried such a variety of traffic that he was naturally drawn to it. This is a May 1965 view, part of a series entitled, and devoted specifically to, "bus stations". Vehicles from the independent Barton, Skill's and South Notts fleet form the backcloth for the Trent Motor Traction Company's Leyland PD2/12 Titan, fleet number **773 (KCH 116)**, which carried an example of the rather spartan Orion body by MCCW. A 59-seater with platform doors, it was withdrawn in 1968.

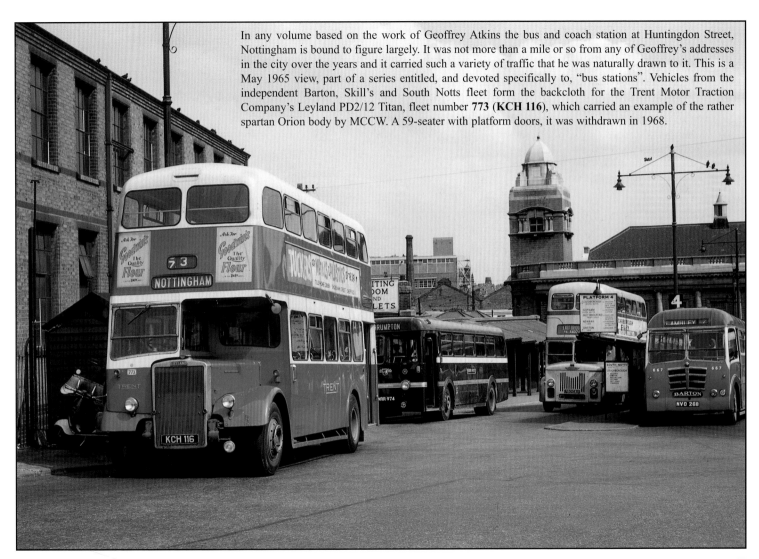

In any poll among those of us who lived through the nineteen-sixties two fleets - City of Oxford and Southdown - would be well up the popularity lists: furthermore, each had a livery among the most attractive to be found.

At the beginning of the decade, in an Oxford scene dating from May 1961, a trio of AECs representing the former operator includes one, No. **715 (NJO 715)**, which was withdrawn later that year. An AEC Regal III, dating from 1949, it carried a Willowbrook 32-seat front-entrance body. It was neatly parked between two Regent V double-deckers: that on the left, with the enclosed radiator, was No. **984 (984 HFC)**, a highbridge 63-seater also bodied by Willowbrook; the other Regent V was No. **184 (WJO 184)** with Park Royal 55-seat lowbridge bodywork; a 1956 machine, it lasted until 1968.

In Brighton in October 1965, the photographer found time to look in at Southdown's Pool Valley bus station. Somewhat cramped, and a place of light and shade, it was nevertheless photogenic, especially during those fleeting hours when the sun was in the right place. Number **785 (RUF 185)** was a Beadle-bodied Leyland Titan PD2/12 with 59 seats and platform doors. New in 1956, it served Southdown for 14 years.

The Birmingham & Midland Motor Omnibus Company's Midland Red fleet was the one of which Geoffrey Atkins took more photographs than any other. It was fascinating, though perhaps strange to an enthusiast not domiciled in its operating area. Much of the strangeness, and appeal, lay in the company's in-house building activities that produced the greater part of its needs for chassis and coachwork.

One of the many appealing features of Geoffrey Atkins's photography is the frequent representation of an operator's vehicles spotted far from its normal operating area. In this case *(above)* a 1954 BMMO C3 coach was at Minehead in June 1965. Number **4237** (**UHA 237**) originally had a Willowbrook 37-seat centre-entrance coach body, replaced in March 1962 with a Plaxton 36-seat front-entrance unit.

In this condition it lasted in the Midland Red fleet until 1970.

Number **5922** (**RHA 922G**) was a single-decker of an altogether different type. A BMMO S23, it had the operator's own bodywork fitted with 51 service-bus seats; it had been new in January 1969, eight months before this September view at Leicester. This bus was withdrawn and scrapped in early 1980.

The vehicles of the North Western Road Car Company Limited, based at Charles Street, Stockport, were often seen by the photographer on long-distance services running to or through his home city, as well as during his frequent trips to Manchester, when Lower Mosley Street coach station was always on the itinerary. By the time of Geoffrey's 1960s colour work, North Western's elderly Bristol chassis had given way to modern 36-feet-long single-deckers and low-height double-deckers, in the latter case including some to the traditional half-cab design.

In the picture above, taken at Huntingdon Street bus station in August 1968, North Western's Alexander-bodied 49-seater No. **909** (**VDB 909**), a Leyland PSU3/1R Leopard, had a good load on for Blackpool. A small boy is anxiously looking through the window, perhaps impatient for the driver's return and the resumption of the journey to the seaside.

Almost at the end of the decade, in May 1969, a visit to Manchester produced this shot *(right)* of one of North Western's AEC Renowns. Number **125 (AJA 125B)** was about to leave on service 6 to Glossop. Passing in 1972 to the SELNEC PTE, several of this batch of Renowns escaped into further service, but this one was scrapped in 1977.

In common with not a few other operators, North Western was cautious in the 1960s in embracing the rear-engined concept for double-deckers, although such vehicles had been available from 1959: the middle of the decade, as we have seen, saw new front-engined AEC Renowns. With hindsight this can be seen to have been a sensible policy, for the earlier examples of rear-engined buses were far from trouble free: London

Transport, indeed, albeit with their unique operating conditions, had considerable difficulties with such vehicles delivered as late as 1965/6.

North Western took some Daimler Fleetlines in 1965. In another May 1969 picture at Lower Mosley Street one of them, No. **189** (**DDB 189C**), displays its handsome, pleasingly rounded Alexander bodywork, so much more attractive than the more boxlike effusions from some other

coachbuilders. The vehicle passed to SELNEC and survived into 1978.

With a similar livery to that of North Western, Trent's Leyland Titan PD3/4 No. **413** (**LRC 447**), a 1958 Willowbrook-bodied 73-seater with platform doors, was at rest *(right)* between trips on the 62 to Mansfield. It was at Huntingdon Street in June 1964. A driver in the background looks wonderingly at the photographer.

Trent was one of the British Electric Traction group of companies to take the Saunders-Roe (SARO) single-deck bus body for underfloor-engined chassis in the nineteen-fifties. Saunders-Roe had built many double-deck bodies for London Transport's RT class; its coachwork was a quality product, of attractive appearance, and it was a pity that the company was forced out of business following its parent company's difficulties arising out of its aircraft building activities. This example *(above)* was on a Leyland Tiger Cub PSUC1/1 chassis. Number **361** (**FCH 11**), which had originally been numbered 812, was at Derby in September 1965. It was withdrawn from service later that year and sold to the Welsh independent, Llynfi, of Maesteg.

That popular-motoring icon of the decade under review, the Morris Minor, in the rarer convertible form, locally registered and with chrome gleaming, follows Trent's Daimler CRG6LX Fleetline No. **480** (**ECH 480C**) at Redhill, north of Nottingham, in September 1965. This Alexander-bodied 78-seater was newly into service. It was renumbered as 980 in October 1977 and was withdrawn from the Trent fleet in 1979. After withdrawal it found further use as a staff bus with Silentnight, of Barnoldswick.

The Trent vehicles illustrated on this pair of pages, although looking like coaches, were in that "neither flesh nor fowl" category known as "dual-purpose". The distinction between luxury coaches and service buses had been becoming less clear-cut through the 1950s and into the 1960s. Vehicle designs increasingly gave scope for specifications that allowed operators to use a new vehicle for its first few years of life as a coach on long-distance routes, and then to downgrade it to service-bus status with a minimum of alteration: indeed, often the only change was to the livery.

Trent's No. **170 (VCH 170)**, a Leyland PSUC1/2 Tiger Cub *(above)*, had Willowbrook 41-seat dual-purpose coachwork. New in 1961, it almost exactly matched the decade and was withdrawn in 1970. It worked for its subsequent owner, Pritchard, of Bethesda, longer than it had done for Trent, running for them from 1972 to 1982. The bodywork is attractive, set off by the livery, but its origins as a service-bus, rather than a coach, shell are evident.

Trent's No. **251 (ECH 251C)** was a later and longer version of the same theme. A 1965 Leyland PSU3/1R Leopard, its Willowbrook coachwork had 51 seats. This one was withdrawn and sold for scrap in 1980.

To add to the confusion over these classifications, Trent's Leyland PSUC1/11 Tiger Cub No. **102 (HRC 102C)**, was when new regarded as a coach despite its Alexander 41-seat body having power-operated folding doors. In this April 1966 scene *(above)* - another at Huntingdon Street bus station, Nottingham - the other buses visible are all from the Trent fleet. One wonders what service the Ford Cortina was operating.

The fleet of Trent's near neighbour, East Midland Motor Services Limited, was a great favourite of both photographer and writer. By the time Geoffrey Atkins was recording its vehicles in colour, East Midland had adopted a rather unimaginative all-over red, not always relieved by lighter bands, in place of yellow, brown and cream, which it had inherited from United Automobile Services when it was an associate of

United in the 1920s. The new livery was, by chance, not so far removed from United's contemporary Tilling red and cream. The blandness of the livery is well shown on No. **D195 (PNN 195F)** *(right)*, which was a 1968 74-seat Alexander-bodied Leyland Atlantean, photographed in 1969. After being renumbered as 295 in May 1978, this bus was withdrawn in 1981 and sold for scrap in 1982.

The bus/coach classification was further complicated by the painting of service buses in a revised livery - usually the service-bus colours reversed - and their use on long-distance services, suggesting that they were regarded as "dual-purpose" in their availability. In a Mansfield picture *(above)* taken in September 1965, a 1961 East Midland Leyland L1 Leopard with Willowbrook 45-seat service-bus bodywork is illustrated in such a reversed livery. It was withdrawn in 1976 and scrapped in 1977.

In 1954 East Midland placed into service a batch of 25 Leyland PSUC1/1 Tiger Cubs fitted with Saunders-Roe 44-seat bus bodies. They were Nos R321-45 (ORR 321-45). These were just early enough to be painted in the yellow and brown livery, but soon succumbed to the all-over red introduced in 1955.

In an April 1962 picture at Mansfield, one of the batch - No. **R333 (ORR 333)** - basks in the sunlight on the depot forecourt. The SARO coachwork was to a pleasing, harmonious design that survived the drab livery well: the restrained use of aluminium beading strips obviously helped. A later variation was to paint the window surrounds cream, which improved the appearance considerably.

A further pair of East Midland pictures from the mid-sixties gives another comparison between outwardly similar vehicles, which were nonetheless differently classified according to their perceived usage. Both are 36 feet long, and they are identically liveried in a variation of the operator's reversed colours.

Further variation - not immediately evident except to the eye of the well-versed enthusiast - can be found in the different chassis makers and coachbuilders.

Number **L428** (**FVO 428D**) *(above)* was a Leyland PSU3/3R Leopard, fitted with 53-seat service-bus bodywork constructed by Weymann's, of Addlestone, and finished at the Elmdon plant of the Metropolitan Cammell Carriage & Wagon Company, after Weymann's closure. New in May 1966, the vehicle was withdrawn in 1978. It was photographed in Regent Street, Nottingham, in June 1969.

Number **C276** (**276 UVO**) *(right)* was an AEC Reliance with Willowbrook dual-purpose 49-seat coachwork, new in May 1964 and withdrawn in 1976. It later ran for the Clynnog and Trevor Motor Company, which still operates in the new Millennium. This photograph was taken at Skegness in September 1964.

The East Yorkshire fleet is very popular with enthusiasts, and is among both writer's and photographer's favourites: again, an unusual and striking, immaculately kept livery has much to do with that, as does the unique roof outline of much of the double-deck fleet from the classic period, needed because many of the company's routes passed beneath the ancient North Bar, an arched exit from the town of Beverley, until revised routings became available as a result of redevelopment.

The stage-carriage fleet was painted in dark blue (at times this appeared black) and cream with a partly white roof. Coaches had an equally attractive scheme of light-blue and cream, as shown on No. **767 (9767 RH)**, a Willowbrook-bodied 47-seat Leyland PSU3/1R Leopard, seen *(above)* at Woodthorpe in September 1964.

The service buses in the East Yorkshire fleet were usually Leylands until, in 1956, the company switched its orders to AEC beginning with some Regent Vs fitted with Willowbrook 56-seat bodies. They had platform doors and, despite only 7.7 litres under the bonnet, are recalled as sprightly performers on the Hull to Scarborough run. Number **640 (VKH 40)** was at Westwood, Scarborough *(right)* in July 1963.

Most East Yorkshire Leyland double-deckers would find a place in any "classic" listing; perhaps the ultimate development of the "Beverley Bar" machine appeared in 1950 with what local enthusiasts always referred to as the "LAT PD2s". These fine machines, often used by the writer on journeys to and from school, were eight-feet-wide Titan PD2/3s with handsome Roe 54-seat - soon increased to 56 - bodywork.

Number **527** (**LAT 55**) *(above)* typifies East Yorkshire's carefully applied traditional livery, with its three cream bands, white U-shaped stripe around the front four-fifths of the roof, cream wheels and destination-screen frame. It was at Scarborough's Westwood bus station in August 1965, waiting to leave for Bridlington, some 20 miles down the coast, shortly before it was withdrawn from service and sold for scrap.

Two years earlier, during another of Geoffrey Atkins's frequent holidays in Scarborough, and parked a matter of yards from the Titan in the previous picture, Hebble Motor Services No. **195** (**PCP 803**) was in Westwood bus station *(right)*. An AEC Reliance dating from 1962, it carried 43-seat service-bus bodywork by Alexander. In April 1971 it passed to Halifax Corporation as No. 123 and served as a driver-trainer for a few months.

Many visits by train to Yorkshire saw impressive coverage built up of Yorkshire Woollen District and Yorkshire Traction vehicles on local services; they were also seen passing through such centres as Derby and Nottingham on express work, and on private hire at Scarborough and Skegness.

There was a certain, stylish *je ne sais quoi* about the coachwork of Thomas Harrington, of Hove, especially when treated to the restrained liveries of the company operators. Yorkshire Woollen's No. **426** - originally 854 - (**EHD 968**) was a combination of Harrington 41-seat coach bodywork and AEC Reliance chassis. The ensemble dated from 1960. It was transferred to Hebble in June 1970 and sold in 1972. It was photographed *(above)* at Nottingham in June 1968, accompanied by 36ft-long coaches from the United Counties, West Yorkshire and East Yorkshire fleets. Number **952** (**EHE 50**) in the Yorkshire Traction fleet *(right)* was a Leyland PD2/12 Titan fitted with Leyland's own lowbridge bodywork seating 53. New in January 1952, No. 952 served the company for over 16 years until sold for scrap in July 1968. It was at Barnsley in May 1965.

Yorkshire Traction's use of red and cream was not uncommon: perhaps, even, that combination of colours was the most often encountered across the whole range of British operators; on YTC vehicles it seemed rather more attractive than some sixties versions, mainly because of the carefully thought-out application of cream to window and windscreen surrounds, all evidenced in this pair of May 1965 pictures at Barnsley.

The picture above shows No. **1216 (WHE 216)**, a 1962 Leyland PSUC1/2 Tiger Cub. It was fitted with Alexander 45-seat bodywork. The seats were to service-bus specification, despite which the vehicle, when new, had been painted in reversed livery for use on express services at peak periods. Yorkshire Traction did this with a number of batches of new buses for their first year or so in service, after which they would reappear in

service-bus livery. Number 1216 was withdrawn in 1973, was in use as a waiting room by January 1974 and was sold for scrap in September 1976.

The picture at right is of No. **1233 (XHE 233)**, also dating from 1962, a Leyland PSU3/3R Leopard with Willowbrook 54-seat bus bodywork. This vehicle ran until 1974 and after withdrawal from service was sold for scrap in October 1975.

Yorkshire Traction's No. **1297** (**CHE 297C**) *(above)* had an interesting history. A Leyland PSU3/1R Leopard, new in April 1965 fitted with a Willowbrook 53-seat bus body, it was withdrawn in 1977, to be extensively rebuilt by Yorkshire Traction. It was renumbered 386 and reregistered EWB 386V, and re-entered service in October 1979. After its second withdrawal in 1984, it passed to St Peter's, Doncaster, in 1986

and then into preservation in Barnsley in April 1990. In this picture it was leading a trio of YTC vehicles at Barnsley bus station, again in May 1965.

Visits to the operating territory of the Northern General Transport Company by Geoffrey Atkins were not frequent, but on occasion its vehicles were sighted far afield, as in this August 1965 view *(right)* taken at Newark.

Northern's No. **1956** (**MCN 56**) was a 1961 Leyland L2 Leopard with another example of the handsome Harrington Cavalier design of coachwork, in this case seating 37. Converted to a 41-seat bus in 1972, it was withdrawn in 1974. It was to receive a new Plaxton 45-seat coach body in 1976 with Cooper, of Stockton Heath (now part of the Mayne group) and be reregistered PJP 276R.

The points made about the use of simplified liveries, often composed of shades of red and cream, across the United Kingdom are reinforced by these views of vehicles from the fleet of Ribble Motor Services Limited. Obvious details such as fleetnames, fleet and registration numbers and the shape of the destination screen were specifically Ribble, but cover them up and the vehicles illustrated on this page could be from, say, the East Midland fleet. In the sixties there was no standardisation policy regarding liveries such as would come in the following decade with the National Bus Company, but buses were nonetheless beginning to move into the "they all look the same" mode.

Another example of the characteristic Saunders-Roe bodywork is seen *(above)* on Ribble's No. **422 (FCK 854)**, a 44-seater dating from 1954 on the Leyland PSUC1/1 Tiger Cub chassis, photographed at Knott End in May 1967. It was withdrawn in 1968.

Ribble's smart - despite the unimaginative livery - No. **1674 (NRN 574)** was a 1960 Leyland PDR1/1 Atlantean - one of the early ones - with MCCW 72-seat bodywork. Seen *(right)* at Lower Mosley Street, Manchester, the vehicle was withdrawn in 1975 and sold to an independent.

In common with other operators discussed in these pages, Ribble used its standard colours in different proportions to achieve a distinctive image for its vehicles used on coaching and dual-purpose work. The then maximum-length single-decker in the picture above just manages to squeeze into our decade: it was delivered in 1969, after Ribble had become part of the National Bus Company, which began its existence on 1st January of that year. Number **953** (**HRN 953G**) was a Leyland PSU3A/4R Leopard with Plaxton 49-seat coachwork seen on express work at Lower Mosley Street, Manchester, in May 1969. The vehicle passed to National Travel (West) Limited, Manchester, in June 1978 and was withdrawn from that fleet in 1980.

Ribble was among the earliest users of the Leyland Atlantean, buying both lowbridge and highbridge buses and a variant with only 50 seats to a luxurious standard and toilet and kitchen facilities for use on express services such as those from the north-west to London. These could be seen with the Ribble fleetname as well as that of the company's coaching subsidiary, Standerwick. Number **34** (**VFR 376**) was one of the latter. A 1961 purchase, with Weymann's bodywork, it was at Blackpool in June 1967 (*right*).

BET operators, through their Federation, took advantage of the bulk-buying that their considerable purchasing power allowed, which meant that a body design to a standard specification could be ordered in large numbers, often from more than one coachbuilder, for allocation to various individual companies. The Federation standard single-decker in the mid sixties was a 53-seat machine that was adaptable in several ways. The two Ribble Leyland Leopards on these pages illustrate the concept: No. **896** (**ECK 896E**) *(above)*, dating from 1967, was a dual-purpose 49-seater from Marshall, of Cambridge whilst No. **614** (**CCK 614C**), delivered two years earlier, had a 53-seat body to service-bus layout built by MCCW. These vehicles were withdrawn respectively in 1979 and 1982 and both were sold for scrap, although CCK 614C managed to survive as a towing vehicle for about three months before being sent to the breaker's yard. Willowbrook and Weymann's were also among the suppliers of Federation standard coachwork. The livery on the service-bus version omitted any form of relief because it was cheaper to spray paint in a single all-over colour and avoid the need to mask off areas of the panelling to apply a second colour.

The photographer's travels seldom took him across the border into Scotland, which is thus among the least well-covered parts of the United Kingdom mainland in his collection. Scottish vehicles, as with those of Northern General recently discussed, did, however, occasionally show themselves in distant locations on extended tour work, in this case *(above)* in Nottingham on the way to Devon and Cornwall.

The luxurious vehicle involved was Eastern Scottish **YB103A (AFS 103B)**, a 1964 AEC Reliance 470 with an Alexander 38-seat coach body. It was at Huntingdon Street in June 1965. After a 15-year career with Eastern Scottish, this vehicle was converted for use as a driver trainer. It was finally withdrawn and scrapped in 1980.

The south-west of England fared a little better through the medium of the occasional summer holiday, during one of which, in August 1962, this Southern National 41-seat Bristol MW5G was photographed *(right)* in Ilfracombe. The 1958 machine was one of the first MWs, with an Eastern Coach Works design - soon modified - of body that omitted the beading and panelling strip below the windows. The latter was not merely decorative and its omission was the cause of early remedial work on some of these bodies.

The Tilling companies' equivalent of the BET Federation standard was a monopoly on the output of the Eastern Coach Works factory at Lowestoft as well as on that of the chassis builders, Bristol. This situation was not far off coming to an end in the mid sixties, but in the meantime identical buses and coaches, mainly in Tilling red or green, could be seen all over the country. United Counties was one of the green fleets, and these two vehicles, photographed at Huntingdon Street, Nottingham, in 1965, bring in a further variation on the "dual-purpose" theme. Number **252** (**ABD 252B**) *(above)*, a Bristol RELH6G of 1964, had 47 high-backed seats and driver-operated power doors, and was thus classified as a dual-purpose machine, a category given a nod by the extra cream around the windows and windscreen. A similar vehicle behind had more green and less cream. Number **158** (**158 BRP**) *(right)* was a 1962 Bristol MW with the later, modified ECW body design that included the strengthening below the windows *(see pages 42/3)*. It was a 41-seater, also classified as dual-purpose, with again a touch more cream in the livery than normal for this service-bus shell. These buses were withdrawn in 1980 and 1977.

The Lincolnshire Road Car Company's ideas for a 41-seat dual-purpose Bristol MW based on the standard ECW bus shell involved extra beading and a half-and-half application of the Tilling green and cream. Above, at Broad Marsh, Nottingham, was No. **2665 (SBE 503)**, originally 3015 and later 2065, a 1958 delivery. It lasted in service until 1977 after having been converted as a 43-seat service bus in November 1969.

Some variations of livery on Bristol/ECW products in England were to be seen in the Nottingham area in the fleets of Mansfield District, Midland General and Notts & Derby, all members of the nationalised former Balfour Beatty organisation.

WAL 438 was No. **511** in the Mansfield District Traction Company fleet. It ran for 12 years from 1958 to 1970 after which it was sold to

West Riding and by August 1971 was in the yard of the breaker North, Sherburn-in-Elmet. It was a Bristol LD6G Lodekka with Eastern Coach Works 58-seat bodywork incorporating platform doors. The photograph included a Barton double-decker and was taken at Huntingdon Street, Nottingham, in June 1967.

47

The Midland General Omnibus Company's rich blue and cream livery survived the nationalisation of the Balfour Beatty group's passenger transport businesses and was perhaps the most attractive to grace the products of the Bristol and ECW factories after Midland General standardised on them after 1954. Before that it had been applied to a series of AECs and Leylands, such as No. **207** (**KRB 93**), seen above in Nottingham in July 1962. We have seen several examples of the bodies built by Saunders-Roe for underfloor-engined chassis in the 1950s: here is an example of their work from the previous decade; 32 seats were provided in an attractive forward-entrance body mounted on a 1948 Leyland PS1/1 Tiger chassis. Withdrawn in 1963, this bus found further use with the building contractor, Yorkshire Hennebique.

Late winter sunlight illumines the splendid Midland General livery as applied to a standard Bristol/ECW product. In March 1962, at Broad Marsh, Nottingham, No. **488 (526 JRA)** *(right)* was awaiting its departure time for Beauvale Estate, Hucknall, with in the background a fine selection of Barton double-deckers.

In a similarly composed Broad Marsh view *(above)*, from July 1967, the Barton contingent is mainly single-deck. The Eastern Coach Works-bodied Bristol on the Beauvale Estate service is now the Notts & Derby Traction Company's 1953 60-seat highbridge KSW6G No. **302 (SRB 530)**, a vehicle that was renumbered as 402 in 1968 and withdrawn later that year. No disposal details are known, and the bus was probably scrapped.

Notts & Derby Bristol Lodekkas of a later generation are seen in a view of the terminal stands in Friar Lane, Nottingham, taken in August 1968 *(right)*. Brand new FLF6Gs Nos. **302/3 (TRB 569/70F)** were 70-seaters and were waiting to leave for Strelley Lane and Ripley respectively. In 1971 these Notts & Derby vehicles were transferred to Midland General, retaining their fleet numbers.

In a third picture taken at the service F4 departure stand at Broad Marsh (with Barton again present), passengers to the Beauvale Estate in Hucknall had luxurious transport in the shape of Midland General's No. **256** (**25 DRB**), a dual-purpose 43-seat ECW-bodied Bristol MW of 1958. This is a March 1967 picture and the vehicle was withdrawn in 1971. It passed for further service to United Counties.

The National Bus Company was already in existence when Midland General ECW-bodied Bristol VRTSL6G No. **316** (**BNU 680G**) was delivered in 1969. This was fortunately too early for the NBC's corporate livery scheme to have deprived us of the heartening sight of the blue livery on the "instant classic" early, flat-fronted VR. Number 316 was later renumbered as 755. It passed to Trent in 1976 when the Midland

General fleet was merged into that of Trent. The VR was withdrawn by Trent in 1981 and sold for scrap in February 1982 when only 13 years old.

From his earliest days behind a lens in the late 1920s, Geoffrey Atkins was fascinated by the standard designs of the London General Omnibus Company and its successors; on many an LNER and, later, British Railways half-day excursion from Nottingham to London he recorded the latest buses and Green Line coaches on the streets of the Capital. Geoffrey's personal photography there starts with buses on solid tyres and ends with types still running today. One of the strengths of Geoffrey's collection is his night photographs; several were taken in London, though regrettably few are in colour. A fine effort was the October 1965 view *(above)* of Trafalgar Square, with the illuminated National Gallery in the background and Routemaster **RM1745 (745 DYE)** passing through on the 24 from Hampstead Heath to Pimlico (Grosvenor Road).

The London Transport RT was practically everybody's favourite, hence no doubt its recent elevation to "Bus of the Century" in a poll among enthusiasts. This one *(right)* is **RT2125 (KGK 934)** of Merton (AL) garage on a private hire to Bournemouth in June 1966. At this time London Transport was restricted in the distance it could send its buses on such work.

That holiday to Bournemouth in June 1966 produced these two views of units of the Bournemouth Corporation fleet in their smart yellow livery with dark red bands.

Number **144** (**YLJ 144**) *(above)* was a Leyland Titan PD3/1 with 62-seat, dual-doorway, highbridge bodywork by Weymann's. New in 1959, it was fitted with the revised radiator grille seen in the picture in 1964, was withdrawn in 1972 and sold to Blue Line, of Upminster, in 1973. It was photographed at the Alum Chine terminal turning circle for service 17.

Bournemouth's trolleybus network was intensively worked with a smart fleet. This Sunbeam MF2B *(right)*, No. **261** (**WRU 261**), with Weymann's bodywork similar in most respects to that on No. 144, was new in 1958 and scrapped in 1966 when a mere eight years old.

During the years that Eastern Coach Works bus and coach bodywork could be supplied to only the state-owned operators, it was usually to be seen in either red and cream or green and cream livery; there were exceptions, particularly in Scotland and, as we have seen, in the Nottingham area. In Sheffield in the sixties could be seen ECW bodies that were not only in a different livery but were not on Bristol chassis.

In 1961 Sheffield's C fleet ("C" signified ownership by the railway but operation by Sheffield) received five Leyland L2 Leopards with ECW 41-seat coach bodies to a design usually found on the Bristol MW chassis. Number **1180** (**1880 WA**) was brand new in this September 1961 view *(above)*. The A fleet, signifying ownership and operation by Sheffield, included No. **360** (**EWB 360C**), a 1965 Leyland

PDR1/2 Atlantean fitted with Neepsend 72-seat bodywork, photographed in May 1965. The PDR1/2 was an attempt by Leyland to improve on the PDR1/1, which had been beset by unreliability problems since its launch in the late 1950s.

At Milton Street, Nottingham, outside Victoria station on 1st July 1966 Geoffrey Atkins was on hand to record the historic occasion of No. **506** (**KTV 506**), a 1950 BUT, working a special last trolleybus journey *(above)*; the Nottingham trolleybus system had operated for the last time in normal service on the previous day. Leading the trolleybus towards the city centre was AEC Regent V No. **236** (**UTV 236**), a Park Royal-

bodied 61-seater dating from 1956; in the background was 1965 AEC Renown No. **369** (**DAU 369C**).

In another *(right)* from the photographer's splendid "Bus Stations" series, Nottingham City Transport's 1958 Leyland Titan PD2/40 No. **7** (**7 ATO**) stands in Broad Marsh alongside South Notts Leyland-bodied lowbridge PD2/12 Titan No. **57** (**NRR 852**), which had been new in

January 1953. It was not withdrawn until April 1975. Perhaps with ideas of preservation, unfortunately never realised, it was retained until 1980 before being scrapped. Barton single- and double-deckers and a Midland General Bristol Lodekka complete this June 1969 scene, in which few colours of the spectrum are not represented in the liveries.

Nottingham's AEC Renowns were purchased for trolleybus replacement, and in the picture above two of them are seen alongside a surviving trolleybus, No. **594** (**KTV 594**), a 1952 BUT Brush-bodied 70-seater. Approaching the camera is No. **358** (**DAU 358C**), while across the road is No. **372** (**DAU 372C**). Both were delivered in 1965 as part of a batch of 35 with 70-seat bodies by Weymann's, of Addlestone; other Nottingham

Renowns were bodied by Northern Counties. This picture was taken in May 1965.

The AEC Renowns were the last front-engined, half-cab buses to be bought new for the Nottingham fleet: thereafter the Leyland Atlantean and the Daimler Fleetline would be the preferred choices; examples of both had appeared before the Renowns. The first Fleetlines were delivered in 1962, they had Park Royal bodies but

we illustrate *(right)* one of the 1963 batch bodied as 77-seaters by Northern Counties. Number **78** (**78 RTO**) was photographed in August 1964 alongside Notts & Derby's 1953 Bristol KSW6G No. **301** (**SRB 529**), an ECW-bodied 60-seater. Nottingham's No. 78 was withdrawn in 1976, although four of the same batch were rebodied by Northern Counties at that time.

Nottingham's neighbouring local authority, West Bridgford Urban District Council, had one of those compact, neat, beautifully maintained fleets often found with the smaller municipalities. Like the larger fleet next door, West Bridgford's was loyal to the AEC *marque*, usually bought new, but very occasionally from another undertaking, as with No. **19** (**ACP 421**), a 1947 AEC Regent III, which was acquired from Halifax Corporation (it had been fleet number 47 there) in January 1963. In the picture above it is seen in July of that year. A Park Royal-bodied 59-seater, it was withdrawn in 1967, not surviving to be taken over by Nottingham in September 1968. A contemporary that did was No. 3 (**KNN 773**), seen *(right)* as Nottingham No. **169** - though still in West Bridgford livery - in November 1968. A 1947 AEC Regent III with Park Royal 56-seat bodywork, it was withdrawn by Nottingham in 1969 and was scrapped later that year.

The South Notts Bus Company Limited was a small independent operating from Gotham on the outskirts of Nottingham. It would later be swallowed up by Nottingham City Transport, but at the time of these late sixties views was still in its prime, fielding well-maintained colourful buses such as these Leyland double-deckers. **MRR 338** *(above)* was No. **48** in the South Notts fleet: a Leyland-bodied 53-seat lowbridge Titan PD2/12, it had been new in 1951 and would be withdrawn in 1973. It was photographed in July 1967. Two years later No. **82 (82 SVO)** was captured on film *(right)*. This was a 1963 Albion Lowlander LR3 with Northern Counties 71-seat highbridge bodywork, which lasted in South Notts service until December 1981. It was sold two years after that to Rimmer, of Market Harborough.

Barton Transport Limited of Chilwell, Nottinghamshire, was no ordinary independent operator. Even in the early 1950s it claimed a route mileage of approximately 1,000, plus another 12½ thousand miles of holiday and tour route mileage in the UK and on the Continent. And its fleet was the enthusiast's delight: around 300 vehicles, in a splendid livery of two shades of red with cream relief, which included every size of bus and coach on a variety of chassis; some bought new and some built in-house were augmented by a remarkable array of second-hand vehicles. The Barton fleet numbering system left nothing to be desired - at least for the enthusiast - in its simple progression from 1 through 1000 (in 1964) and beyond, with no reuse of numbers.

As that magic 1000 approached there was much speculation as to what it would be: surely something special? And so it was: **ANN 700B** was exhibited in the demonstration park at the 1964 Commercial Motor Show. A Bedford VAL14 with Duple Vega Major 52-seat coachwork, it later took its place as Barton's No. **1000**. It was about two years old in this October 1964 picture *(above)*. It stayed with Barton until October 1973, when it was withdrawn and later sold for further service.

Although Barton made much use of lighter-weight Bedford chassis, there were many heavyweights too. By 1967 the fleet numbers were approaching 1100 and some AEC Reliance 691s were ordered. Plaxton provided the 53-seat coachwork. Here are two of them when brand new, Nos **1093/9** (**LVO 93/9E**), at Skegness in August 1967. Both were withdrawn in 1974.

There was an intake of new Bedfords into the Barton fleet in 1961. These two SB1 models, photographed at Huntingdon Street, Nottingham, in August 1968 *(above)*, were Nos **908/11** (**662 KNN/283 KVO**). Both had 41-seat coach bodies, by Duple on No. 908 and Burlingham on No. 911. Both lasted a creditable ten years in arduous service with Barton and both went on to run for new owners.

The story of Barton's second-hand double-deckers over the years would need a book all to itself. There had been AEC Regents in earlier years, but all had gone by 1967. In March of that year **SAU 199** was bought from Nottingham City Transport with whom it had carried the fleet number 199. Allocated Barton's fleet number **1087**, it was a Park Royal-bodied 53-seat lowbridge Regent III, which had been new to

Nottingham in 1954. Withdrawn by Barton in 1972, it was exported to the USA. It was photographed *(right)* in Nottingham in May 1968.

When London Transport decided that large numbers of its postwar standard double-deckers were surplus to requirements, operators all over the country joined in the rush to acquire them. Barton went in for ex-RTL-class Leylands in some quantity, one of which - ex-London RTL1539 - became Barton No. **1034** (**OLD 648**), added to the fleet at the end of 1965. It was withdrawn after only eighteen months, in June 1967, and became transport for a Nottingham scout group. The picture *(above)* dates from June 1966. Behind the RTL was Midland General Bristol LD6G Lodekka No. **484** (**522 JRA**).

The writer recalls riding on AEC's Bridgemaster demonstrator **76 MME** when it was on demonstration in Kingston-upon-Hull in about 1957, thinking what an attractive vehicle it was, and later feeling that the East Yorkshire production forward-entrance versions were something of a let-down. 76 MME was the fourth Bridgemaster built and was one of no fewer than six used as demonstrators. It was acquired by Barton in 1958 and numbered **805**. It was in Nottingham *(right)* in May 1969. Barton withdrew it in 1972 and it ran for two subsequent owners in Cheltenham until 1976.

In a fleet as varied as that of Barton, it would be difficult to pick out any single type as typical, although perhaps the Duple-bodied Leyland PD1 Titans might qualify. With their lowbridge 55-seat bodywork and twin sliding entrance/exit doors just forward of centre, they could certainly never have been mistaken for anyone else's vehicles. This one *(above)* was No. **474 (HVO 135)**, seen at Huntingdon Street, Nottingham, in July 1967. It had been new in 1947 and survived into 1971. It then passed to a dealer at Arnold, Nottingham, but was quickly resold to a Barnsley scrap dealer.

Another example *(right)* of a second-hand Barton purchase is that of No. **954 (CCK 362)**, a Leyland PD2/3 Titan of 1948, acquired in 1962 and kept until 1967 when it was sold for scrap. The bodywork was built by Leyland to 53-seat lowbridge specification.

On the other hand, sleek 36-feet-long coaches are for some the 'face' of Barton. A particularly attractive example of this category of vehicle was No. **1005** (**BVO 5C**), a 1965 AEC Reliance 590 fitted with Harrington Grenadier 51-seat coachwork. A ride on one of these vehicles on one of Barton's tightly timed long-distance services with a keen driver was an experience not soon forgotten. A September 1969 view.

But maybe, after all, many would regard the heterogeneous collection of second-hand vehicles, expertly overhauled and immaculately presented in that fabulous livery, more often than not sparklingly driven, as the essence of Barton in the decade under discussion. Leicester City Transport disposed of some 1946 Leyland Titan PD1s in 1960, one of which, **DJF 344**, became Barton's No. **877**. A Leyland-bodied highbridge

56-seater, this veteran managed another six years of reliable service before being sold in 1966 for scrap.

Barton watchers were agog when the news broke that the business of Hall Bros, of South Shields, with its Tyneside - Midlands express service, was to be acquired in July 1967. The business was maintained as a separate subsidiary for a while, and some of the vehicles were noted with fleet numbers in a temporary H series. Eventually the fleet was fully integrated and fleet numbers in Barton's sequence allocated. This pair of pictures illustrates Hall Bros coaches in Nottingham before the takeover.

Above is **DCU 585D**, a 1966 Bedford VAL14 with Duple coachwork. Barton sold this vehicle in 1973; later, between September 1977 and February 1978, it was owned by a Stevenage independent. The writer recalls, during a period of income augmentation, driving it on a private hire to the Newmarket area, during which, as it passed over a bump in the road, the complete dashboard jumped out and landed in his lap. The VAL's reputation for going well but not being able to stop was also borne out by personal experience. **KCU 709** was a 1964 Harrington Grenadier-bodied Leyland PSU3/3R Leopard. This one lasted until 1974 after moving to Barton.

The photographs were taken at Huntingdon Street in October 1966 and June 1964.

Demonstrators have always added interest to the public transport scene. Even if without much chance of landing an order, a salesman would hopefully offer a demonstrator for a week or so; sometimes his efforts were rewarded, perhaps against the odds and to his surprise as much as to anybody else's. When AEC Renown **7552 MX** went to Nottingham in September 1963, policy there was already favouring rear-engined buses: Daimler Fleetlines had entered service in 1962/3

and Leyland Atlanteans were on order for 1964 delivery. 7552 MX's visit might thus not have been expected to be very productive. As we have seen, however, a substantial order, perhaps encouraged by reports from the NCT scrutineers visible at the right of the picture, was placed for Renowns to be used as trolleybus replacements.

And here we must take a regretful leave of Geoffrey Atkins and his cameras in colour in the 1960s. GHFA has gone on to watch and record the

changing scene through the following three decades and into the new Century. Readers who have enjoyed this volume will surely welcome the news that a companion on the nineteen-seventies is planned.